2022 9급 전 직렬 공무원 시험 대비

심슨북스

2022
복습종이

구문1000제

효율적 회독 학습을 위한
구문 1000제 복습종이

지은이 **심우철**

2022 NEW

커넥츠 공단기
인터넷 강의 gong.conects.com

Contents

목차

최소시간 X 최대효과
초고효율 심우철 합격영어

PART 03 목적어편

PART 04 보어편

PART 05 준동사편

Contents
목차

PART 07 나머지 세상의 모든 구문   118

부록. 직독직해의 법칙

심우철 구문 1000제 [복습종이]

최소시간 X 최대효과 = 초고효율 심우철 합격영어

PART

01

문장 구조편

PATTERN 01 | 구와 절은 영어의 핵심

❖ 다음을 해석하세요.

구문분석집 10P

01 The invention of the inexpensive microchip has made computers affordable to many people.

02 Social scientists say that this change in the family is one of the important changes from a traditional society to a modern society.

03 Becoming good at handling information is going to be one of the most important skills of the twenty-first century, not just in school but in the real world.

04 Peter Carson, chief executive of Brinksmann, also expects that its new technology for manufacturing small batches of books will enable the new company to sell more books to Spanish speakers in the United States, Canada, and elsewhere.

05 one of the most beguiling aspects of cyber space

[2011년 지방직 9급 3번]

06 the best way of describing the ex-communist region [2011년 국가직 7급 7번]

07 a basic understanding of the different types of cloning [2009년 국가직 7급 13번]

08 the viability of reclaimed water for indirect potable reuse [2011년 국가직 9급 1번]

09 the European political theorists of the eighteenth century [2011년 지방직 7급 8번]

10 a result of cross-fertilization of ideas between people from different parts of the world

[2010년 국회 8급 5번]

11 by synthesizing the different components of the sound waves [2008년 지방직 9급 15번]

12 by measuring the directions to planets at different parts of their orbits [2011년 국가직 7급 16번]

13 reading one of those historical accounts of the emergence of the human species

[2010년 국회 8급 1~2번]

14 their creation of a new family by symbolically sweeping away of their former single lives

[2008년 국가직 9급 12번]

15 To like many people spontaneously and without effort is perhaps the greatest of all sources of personal happiness.

[2011년 국가직 9급 15번]

16 Note-taking is the best way to remember what you were taught or what you have read.

17 Predicting interview questions and thinking about answers in advance will help you feel more confident.

18 The book is invaluable both for the person who plans to make writing a career and for the individual who would like to earn extra money through part-time writing.

19 Since the decipherment of the writing system in the third decade of the last century, the language has been among the most thoroughly researched areas of Egyptology.

20 The number of foreigners interested in the Korean language has increased dramatically over the past few years because of the success of Korean firms overseas and growing interest in Korean culture.

21 The separation of conventional medicine, based on drugs and surgery, and alternative medicine really occurred in the early 20th century.

22 All of us have had the experience of not being able to find the right words to get across our meaning, of being misunderstood, or of finding that we don't make ourselves clear.

23 Unfortunately, however, poor conditions in the urban areas, such as lack of housing, worsening sanitation and unemployment, bring about an increase in poverty, disease and crime.

24 The explosive growth of world-population has not been caused by a sudden increase in human fertility, and probably owes little in any part of the world to an increase in birthrate.

25 In addition, the intense volume of some popular music, especially heavy metal rock music, has resulted in the loss of some or all of the hearing of a few musicians and members of their audiences.

26 According to psychologist Howard Gardner, the traditional view of intelligence as a uniform capacity to solve problems and think logically is not only unfair to those who haven't got it, but it is incorrect.

27 Despite framing the estate tax as an abusive measure targeted at small business owners and family farms, proponents of terminating the estate tax are attempting to shelter the assets of extremely wealthy constituents.

28 The new knowledge and the new techniques developed in biological research over recent decades have slowly begun to provide understanding of human disease and the hope of definitive therapeutic and preventive measures.

29 Persons with great potential ability sometimes fall down on the job because of laziness or lack of interest in the job, while persons with mediocre talents have often achieved excellent results through their industry and their loyalty to the interests of their employers.

30 When the Industrial Revolution broke out in England, its profitableness seemed so immense that the change was welcomed and blessed by the advocates for Progress. While deploring the long hours of labour to which the first generation of the factory workers, including women and children, were condemned, and the sordid conditions of their new life in both factory and home, the admirers of the Industrial Revolution were confident that these were temporary evils which could and would be removed.

❖ 다음을 해석하세요.

구문분석집 18P

01 Pine seedling grown in pots of soil sterilized by humans died within two or three years of being planted in the ground.

02 One time a person on my team came to me with a problem that she was having at work.

03 The front pages of newspapers tell of the disintegration of the social fabric, and the resulting atmosphere of anxiety in which we all live.

04 There still remain many issues to be resolved even after her lifelong devotion to the poor and helpless in this obscure village.

[2011년 지방직 9급 1번]

05 Increased leisure and the lack of outlet for violent instincts in modern urban life made for an aimless type of violence among teenagers, which aroused emotional sympathy among intellectuals.

06 When he retires, Professor Jones will have been teaching here for over thirty years, but his classes are never dull.

PATTERN 03 | S + V + SC

❖ 다음을 해석하세요.

구문분석집 20P

01 Jupiter is the fifth planet from the Sun and the biggest planet of the solar system.

02 At that time he was not yet married, but got married two years later.

03 The young girl felt accustomed to living in the new society and got taught a lot of customs and manners.

04 The greatest barriers to high level of performance or reaching your potential are mental barriers that we impose upon ourselves.

05 A keen consciousness on the part of the general public as to the role of the newspaper is a prerequisite to the successful maintenance of a democratic society.

06 The first impression given by the clothes many young people wear these days for any and all occasions is one of conformity and uniformity as if they felt obliged to adorn themselves in the same style.

07 The lasting fascination of the Robinson Crusoe myth is due to its attempt to imagine an individual independent of society.

PATTERN 04 ㅣ S + V + O

❖ 다음을 해석하세요.

구문분석집 22P

01 Effective analysis and recognized techniques can bring about a great improvement.

02 The democratic ideals of the young country demanded direct responsibility to the people and a direct benefit to society.

03 The period of quarantine depends on the amount of time necessary for protection against the spread of a particular disease.

04 However, a month later, the U.S. Olympic committee took away his medals because Thorpe had played baseball for money.

05 The Vietnamese Communist regime, long weakened by regionalism and corruption, can barely control the relentless destruction of the country's forests.   [2009년 지방직 7급 6번]

06 According to interviews in a *Ms*. magazine with women who have undergone breast implant surgery, many women felt effects like crippling fatigues, joint pain, and irritable skin which leads to skin rashes.   [2010년 국가직 7급 4번]

07 Similarly, many physicians were recommending daily vitamin E supplements to lower heart disease risk, but results of a recent study showed possible cause for concern, since the group taking vitamin E supplements had high risks of hospitalization for heart failure.

❖ 다음을 해석하세요.

구문분석집 24P

01 Our culture teaches us what to pay attention to and what to ignore. It also teaches us when to smile or look serious.

02 An Eskimo once told European visitors that the only true wisdom lives far from mankind, out in the great loneliness.

03 My wife has always asked me if I loved her when we got married.

04 Many people stop at least once in their lives to ask themselves what their lives are all about and whether they are living well.

05 He should then read the schoolchildren what was said by the newspapers on one side, what was said by those on the other, and some fair account of what really happened.

06 New research has shown people that early childhood experiences do not just create a background for development and learning, but they directly affect the way the brain is wired.

07 Any experienced parent will tell you that the best way to get a broccoli-hating child to sample this food is to have another child sitting nearby who enthusiastically is eating broccoli.

PATTERN 06 I S + V + O + OC

❖ 다음을 해석하세요.

구문분석집 26P

01 The noise of heavy traffic will also make the town less attractive, and life in Springfield will be less pleasant than it was before.

02 The recent increase of the labor cost and tax in Korea has forced both large enterprises and small and medium enterprises to move into China.

03 A rapid increase in the number of college graduates has made the competition for jobs much greater than it used to be.

04 Lastly, in the 20th century, the shift in population from the countryside to the cities made schools more concerned with social problems. [2008년 국가직 7급 11번]

05 In the face of an uncooperative Congress, the President may find himself impotent to accomplish the political program to which he is committed.

06 The most important thing for you to do as a student of literature is to advise yourself to be an honest student, for in the intellectual sphere at any rate honesty is definitely the best policy.

07 We have thereby been enabled to make conditions of human existence incomparably more favorable in numerous respects, but in our enthusiasm over our progress in knowledge and power we have arrived at a defective conception of civilization itself.

PATTERN 07 | 그 밖의 문장 형식

❖ 다음을 해석하세요.

구문분석집 28P

01 The accident deprived me of the pleasure of baseball.

02 She furnished him with the facts surrounding the case.

03 She placed the eggs in some cold water for half an hour to cool them.

04 The rain prevented them from eating outdoors.

05 That evening, just as we passed the mouth of the Potomac River, the US Coast Guard warned all ships of imminent severe weather and said to seek safe harbor.

06 Internet advertisements can not only raise awareness about goods or services, but they can also provide consumers with additional information on demand.

07 All of this is leading us to a better understanding of how hormones control growth in animals, including humans.

08 Though her actor father discouraged all of his kids from becoming child actors, she began going to auditions while in high school.

09 Aung San Suu Kyi, the Burmese dissident, was under house arrest in 1991 and it prohibited her from traveling to Norway to accept her Nobel Peace Prize.

10 After a brief economic bonanza in the early 1990s that filled Buenos Aires with glitz, the most severe economic crisis in Argentina's history pushed half the population below the poverty level.

[2011년 국회 8급 2번]

문장 구조의 기본 형태

PATTERN 08 | 핵심어 + 수식어 (직독직해의 핵심)

❖ 다음을 해석하세요.

구문분석집 31P

01 Do you know the woman sitting in front of the building?

02 Hearing about a dinosaur alive in the rain forests of South America, a professor launches a scientific expedition.

03 Because of oil products, we can make light engines, which enable airplanes to rise into the air and automobiles to speed along highways.

04 Today the number of workers who go on strike for higher wages is almost twice that of twenty years ago.

05 Egypt last month ordered the slaughter of all poultry kept in homes, as part of efforts to stop the spread of the bird flu virus.

06 At night, schools of prey and predators are almost always spectacularly illuminated by the bioluminescence produced by the microscopic and larger plankton. [2010년 국회 8급 3~4번]

07 The *Harry Potter* series of novels has been the subject of a number of legal proceedings, largely stemming from claims by the American religious groups that the magic in the books promotes witchcraft among children.

08 The Castle Green Condominium management committee has been pasting lists of residents' names on notice boards next to letter-boxes and in elevators at the blocks where they live, including the amounts — ranging from over $1,000 to $10,000 — they owed, reported *The New Paper* on Tuesday. [2010년 서울시 9급 10번]

09 The Vietnamese Communist regime, long weakened by regionalism and corruption, can barely control the relentless destruction of the country's forests, which are home to some of the most spectacular wild species in Asia, including the Java rhinoceros, dagger-horned goats, as well as newly discovered animals previously unknown to Western science. [2009년 지방직 7급 6번]

PATTERN 09 | 문장 요소가 생략되는 경우 (생략 공통 구문)

❖ 다음을 해석하세요.

구문분석집 34P

01 Those who know themselves are wise; those who didn't are not.

02 Thus, the youth may identify with the aged, one gender with the other, and a reader of a particular limited social background with members of a different class or a different period.

03 What if there were no air!

04 He is not and will not be what he used to be.

05 According to ancient lore, every man is born into the world with two bags suspended from his neck — one in front and one behind, and both are full of faults.

06 For instance, in warmer areas the sandal was, and still is, the most popular form of footwear, whereas the modern moccasin derives from the original shoes adopted in cold climates by races such as Eskimos and Siberians.

07 Although both deal with negotiation, a mediator needs to maintain neutrality and an advocate partiality in order to avoid crossing over into each other's role.

08 No matter how near the dawn was or how weary the man, classes had to be prepared. The student might be forgiven for coming to class unprepared; the teacher never.

09 There is a general apathy, if not positive distrust, of science itself as a search for truth; for, to the ordinary American, science is identified with mechanical inventions.

10 There is an almost peculiar correlation between what is in front of our eyes and the thoughts we are able to have in our heads: large thoughts at times requiring large views, new thoughts new places.

11 In many Western countries, there are still differences in the curricula girls and boys follow — home economics or domestic science being studied by the one, for example, woodwork or metalwork by the other.

PATTERN 10 | 문장 요소의 위치가 변하는 경우 (도치 구문)

❖ 다음을 해석하세요.

구문분석집 38P

01 Not only does the act of writing a note like this focus your attention on what's right in your life, but the person receiving it will be touched and grateful.

02 Behind the clouds is the sun still shining.

03 In Pamplona, a white-walled, sun-baked town high up in the hills of Navarre, is held in the first two weeks of July each year the World's Series of bull fighting.

04 Among them were some tulips, and out of one of these, as it opened, flew a bee.

05 Only in the earliest times, when there were very few humans about, may this not have been true.

06 Not only does the 'leaf fish' look like a leaf, but it also imitates the movement of a drifting leaf underwater.

07 So sudden was the attack that we had no time to escape.

08 So great is the force of tornadoes that they elevate trains off their tracks.

09 Looking back, it seems most odd that never once in all the years that I was at school was there any general discussion about careers.

10 Among interesting things to observe as you travel around the world are the varied ways in which people conduct themselves at parties.

11 The settlement of America was a unique experience in the history of man. Never before in recorded times had a whole culture — in this case, the culture of Western Europe — been transferred bodily to another and previously unknown continent.

PATTERN 11 | 「형용사 + be동사 + S」 / 「형용사, S + V」 / 「of 명사, S + V」가 나온 경우

❖ 다음을 해석하세요.

구문분석집 41P

01 Most helpful to the calm and peaceful atmosphere that the two-year-old child needs but cannot produce for himself/herself is the presence of comforting music, in almost any form.

02 Of the 300 to 400 people who die every day in our country as a result of smoking, many are young smokers.

03 More important than success, which generally means promotion or an increase in salary, is the happiness which can only be found in doing work that one enjoys for its own sake and not merely for the rewards it brings.

04 Included in the art collection are sixteen photographs of the painter John Sloan.

05 Injuries may harm a football player physically, but worse than the physical discomfort they create is the psychological damage they sometimes bring.

06 Of all the ways that automobiles damage the urban environment and lower the quality of life in big cities, few are as maddening and unnecessary as car alarms.

07 So weird were the events surrounding the two murders that even an elaborate official investigation conducted by Chief Justice Warren could not quiet all doubts and theories about what had really happened. [2009년 지방직 7급 7번]

08 Of all the characteristics of ordinary human nature envy is the most unfortunate; not only does the envious person wish to inflict misfortune and do so whenever he can with impunity, but he is also himself rendered unhappy by envy.

심우철 구문 1000제 [복습종이]

최소시간 X 최대효과 = 초고효율 심우철 합격영어

PART

02

주어편

주어의 기본 형태

PATTERN 12 | 「준동사 / 명사구 / 명사절 + V」가 나온 경우

1.「To RV / RVing / 명사구 + V」가 나온 경우

❖ 다음을 해석하세요.

구문분석집 46P

01 To think of the future in relation to the present is essential to civilization.

02 As the custom of going somewhere in the summer has become general, every good mother's care for her children makes her long to take them to the sea.

03 Being a good observer and reactor means being attentive and sensitive to other people's cues, in both their facial and body language.

04 In the age of abundance, the apparent availability of virtually all material necessities tended to lead people to expect speedy gratification of their desires.

05 Breaking deeply embedded habitual tendencies such as procrastination, impatience, criticalness, or selfishness that violate basic principles of human effectiveness involves more than a little willpower and a few minor changes in our lives.

06 Being able to record and predict such events as the ripening of berries, fruits, and grasses, as well as the migration periods of different birds, fish, and game animals, greatly improved the potential for survival of these early human beings and made it possible for them to plan for the first time in human history.

2. 「명사절 + V」가 나온 경우

❖ 다음을 해석하세요.

구문분석집 48P

01 Whether he is rich or poor makes no difference to me.

02 What a person thinks on his own without being stimulated by the thoughts and experiences of other people is at best insignificant and monotonous.

03 Whether the text will unfold new meanings to him depends upon a man's knowledge and experience of life.

04 What you are asking of high schoolers is to keep track of five or six subjects, plan ahead for their long term projects, and decide what is important to study.

05 That any other business is better than the one in which they are engaged is a prevalent idea among men who are not very prosperous in their occupation.

PATTERN 13 | 「S + 준동사 / 부사구 / 관계사절 + V」가 나온 경우

1. 「S + to RV / RVing / p.p. / 부사구 + V」가 나온 경우

❖ 다음을 해석하세요.   구문분석집 50P

01 Americans in the process of creating a land of abundance began to judge themselves by materialistic standards.

02 The most common mistake made by amateur photographers is that they are not physically close enough to their subjects.

03 Education promoting coping-skills and realistic strategies for dealing with stress is important in helping young people recognize that problems can be confronted, though not necessarily solved.

04 North Korea's public food stocks, already exhausted in some parts of the hunger-stricken country, would have run out by June 20, a U.N. official said Tuesday.

05 The evidence so far collected by archaeologists and paleontologists suggests that the cradle of humankind was in East Africa, about five million years ago, when the Australopithecines first appeared. [2011년 지방직 7급 10번]

2. 「S + 관계사절 + V」가 나온 경우

❖ 다음을 해석하세요. 구문분석집 51P

01 One of the most common questions that I am asked by email is why Alan Greenspan's remarks are so important for the behavior of the stock market.

02 People who are still not familiar with the computerized catalog have to make several telephone calls or make several car trips to find out the books they need.

03 Everything that the businessman discussed with the book editor last night was proven to be false by the investigative reporter from the national television network.

04 A businessman who is frustrated by stage fright whenever he must address a conference may devote special efforts to overcoming this handicap and consequently may become an outstanding public speaker.

05 The man who likes chess sufficiently to look forward throughout his working day to the game that he will play in the evening is fortunate, but the man who gives up work in order to play chess all day has lost the virtue of moderation.

06 Children in centers that had more portable playground toys and other characteristics showing support for active playtime reported about 80 more minutes of moderate to vigorous physical activity and 140 fewer minutes of sedentary activity each week compared to centers that were viewed as less supportive of physical activity.

[2008년 국가직 7급 18번]

PATTERN 14 | 「It be + 형·명 + to RV / that절」이 나온 경우

❖ 다음을 해석하세요.

구문분석집 54P

01 It is regrettable that few people should walk today because of the development of traffic facilities.

02 It is certainly believed that the function of school is to produce knowledgeable people.

03 It is more likely that a small-to-medium size school would give them the benefits of both individual attention and practical learning.

04 I always think it is sad to visit high schools and see groups of teens hurry after school for smoking, as if they were waiting all day for it. [2010년 국회 8급 6번]

05 It has been calculated that people who worked in cities during the 1990s spent the equivalent of three whole years of their lives battling through the rush-hour traffic on their way to and from work.

06 It has been suggested that environment is the predominant factor in the incidence of drug addiction, but recent studies with twins separated at birth indicate that a predisposition to addiction can be inherited.

07 "It is an odd fact," notes the social historian Alan Jenkins, "that in war, when people are so busy prosecuting hostilities that they should theoretically have no time to read, they somehow find time to read more than they ever read in peace."

08 It is a fact of social history that those things which are regarded as luxuries in one period do not appear so in another period, that a comfort which is extended only to a particular class as an exceptional right will later appear as a necessity for everyone.

09 Since our democratic system of government is based on representation, and effective representation in turn depends on communication between candidates and voters, it is clear that the success of our form of government depends to a great extent upon the use of language.

PATTERN 15 | 「It ~ that」 강조 구문

❖ 다음을 해석하세요.

구문분석집 57P

01 It was Peter that my aunt took to London yesterday, not Lucy.

02 It is the act of believing that is the starting force or generating action that leads great men and women to accomplishment.

03 It is as a pupil and admirer that I stand at the grave of the greatest man who taught me in college.

04 It is our parents who have given us our sense of right and wrong, our understanding of love, and our knowledge of who we are.

05 It was the gradual transition from hunting and gathering to agriculture that opened up new possibilities for cultural development.

06 It is when you are superior to your previous self that you are truly praiseworthy.

07 It is not so much what a man wears as the way he wears it that marks the born gentleman. The same can be said of a woman; it is the manner in which her clothes are worn that distinguishes a true lady.

08   Very, very early in my boyhood I had acquired the habit of going about alone to amuse myself in my own way, and it was only after years, when my age was about twelve, that my mother told me how anxious this singularity in me used to make her.

09   It is because particular individuals, fortunate in situation or in abilities, are able to take advantage of uncertainty and ignorance, and also because for the same reason big business is often a lottery, that great inequalities of wealth come about.   [2010년 국가직 9급 18번]

PATTERN 16 | It이 주어로 쓰이는 다양한 표현

❖ 다음을 해석하세요.   구문분석집 60P

01   It is raining in the mountains.

02   It is twenty miles from here to Seoul Station.

03   It was long before I realized that the only thing that mattered to me in a work of art was what I thought about it.

04 If a book does not interest us, it does not follow that the fault is in the book.

05 It may be that animals have some special sense that tells them of coming weather.

06 It was not long before each of us in the dorm felt that this man who was every plant's best friend was our friend, too.

07 If you ask people what animals they hate or fear most, chances are you will hear the following: skunks, bats, snakes and rats. [2008년 국가직 7급 20번]

PATTERN 17 | 무생물 주어가 나온 경우

❖ 다음을 해석하세요. 구문분석집 62P

01 A loud report of a gun in the street brought her to the window of the cafe.

02 Our first meeting was at an obscure library, where the accident of our both being in search of the same very rare volume brought us into closer communion.

03   A child who is lost is still advised to find a policeman, but the sight of a police officer no longer creates a feeling of reassurance.

04   Luck or the grace of Heaven may seem to take part in many happenings in life, but a little deeper looking into the causes of them reveals that one's own efforts were by far more responsible for them than most people imagine.

05   A slender acquaintance with the world must convince every man that actions, not words, are the true standard of judging the attachment of friends, and that the most liberal professions of good-will are very far from being the surest marks of it.

06   In the age of abundance, the apparent availability of virtually all material necessities tended to lead people to expect speedy gratification of their desires and to have little sense of the length of time over which people in other times and places had had to wait in order to have some of their more basic material needs satisfied.

심우철 구문 1000제 [복습종이]

최소시간 X 최대효과 = 초고효율 심우철 합격영어

PART

03

목적어편

심우철 구문 1000제 [복습종이]

목적어의 기본 형태

PART 03 목적어편

PATTERN 18 | 「V + 준동사 / 명사구 / 명사절 / 명사 + 수식어」가 나온 경우

1. 「V + to RV / RVing / 명사구」가 나온 경우

❖ 다음을 해석하세요.

구문분석집 66P

01 I regret to inform you that I am giving four weeks' notice of my resignation from the company.

02 The great English historian had perhaps the most remarkable memory.

03 Many women began realizing the role and images forced upon them by a male-dominated society and started to do something about it.

04 New therapies include inactivating damaged genes and boosting the immune system's ability to destroy cancerous cells.

[2008년 국가직 7급 19번]

05 Contrary to those museums' expectations, however, he has decided to retain permanent control of his works in an independent foundation that makes loans to museums rather than give any of the art away.

[2010년 지방직 7급 5번]

2. 「V + 명사절」이 나온 경우

❖ 다음을 해석하세요.

구문분석집 67P

01 We will find out who is going to be named champion.

02 Most of the board members cannot decide whether they will continue with the project or start over with some fresh ideas, like your plan for the intersection at Main and Fifth Street.

03 I cannot help but regret how little I am able to contribute to the discussion of the many debatable questions.

04 A Melbourne study of 6,000 people showed that owners of dogs and other pets had lower cholesterol, blood pressure and heart attack risk compared with people who didn't have pets.

[2009년 국가직 9급 14번]

05 In recent years, the U.S. Environmental Protection Agency(EPA) has argued that many carcinogens that are known to have a one-in-a-million chance of inducing cancer may be categorized as "chemicals that pose a minimal hazard." [2010년 지방직 7급 17번]

06 When Thomas Edison proclaimed in 1922 that the motion picture would replace textbooks in schools, he began a long string of spectacularly wrong predictions regarding the capacity of various technologies to revolutionize teaching. [2010년 서울시 9급 6번]

3. 「V + 명사 + 수식어」가 나온 경우

❖ 다음을 해석하세요.

구문분석집 69P

01 We simply do not have the technology to travel to the nearest star in a human lifetime.

02 Our incredible growth rate leads to a continuous recruitment of ambitious programmer analysts who have the desire to make a significant contribution to an expanding company.

03 Greek and Chinese inventors made clever moving statues that could duplicate the actions of a person or animal, such as playing a musical instrument or flapping wings and crowing.

[2011년 국회 8급 9번]

04 Active euthanasia means that a physician or other medical personnel takes a deliberate action that will induce death. Passive euthanasia means letting a patient die for lack of treatment or suspending treatment that has begun.

[2010년 국가직 9급 14번]

PATTERN 19 | 「O + S + V」/「S + V + OC + O」가 나온 경우

❖ 다음을 해석하세요.

구문분석집 70P

01 What would be the outcome of the contest nobody knew.

02 He made possible an instrument of destruction with which the earth could be totally disfigured.

03 No word was spoken, but the wide variety of gestures made clear to everyone what the performer was saying.

04 Machines have made possible the mass production of all kinds of goods.

05 How many minutes had passed the child did not know, but he suddenly found a little girl standing before him.

06 The only way in which social life can continue is for each individual to keep unimpaired his or her own independence and self-respect as well as that of others.

07 There is a deep-rooted tendency to dislike, to distrust, and to regard as inferior individuals or groups speaking a language different from one's own just as one considers the monkey a lower animal because it has no language at all.

PATTERN 20 | 가목적어-진목적어의 해석

❖ 다음을 해석하세요.

구문분석집 72P

01 I found it really enjoyable to ride a snowboard in winter.

02 Having a driver's license makes it easy for teenagers to go out to parties, movies, and malls.

03 It is up to you to abolish war and to see to it that the necessities of life are made available to all mankind.

04 Because of his somnolent voice, the students find it difficult to concentrate in his classes.

[2010년 지방직 7급 13번]

05 We should not, therefore, attempt to abolish competition, but only to see to it that it takes forms which are not too injurious.

06 Meanwhile, the underlying problem remains unaddressed and may worsen, and the side effects of the symptomatic solution make it still harder to apply the fundamental solution.

07 The problem is that when nutrients are studied in isolation, we ignore the vastness of the system as a whole, making it extremely difficult to know what any given nutrient's effect really is within the system.

08 Rather, the best way to bring out one's mature empathic potential is through induction, in which parents highlight the other's perspective, point up the other's distress, and make it clear that the child's action caused it.

09 The automobile has made it possible for father to work a considerable commuting time away from home, so he often rises before the children do and sees them only for a brief period on his return from work and during the weekends.

심우철 구문 1000제 [복습종이]

최소시간 X 최대효과 = 초고효율 심우철 합격영어

PART

04

보어편

보어의 기본 형태

PATTERN 21 | 보어에 「명사(구) / 형용사 / 준동사」가 나온 경우

1. 보어에 「명사 / 형용사 / 명사 + 수식어」가 나온 경우

❖ 다음을 해석하세요.

구문분석집 78P

01 One man's terrorist is another man's freedom fighter.

02 He seemed very grateful to Crusoe for having saved his life, and as he appeared willing
to accompany him, Crusoe took him home as a servant.

03 Since basalt is formed under extremely high temperatures, the presence of this type of
rock is an indication that the temperature of the Moon was once extremely hot.

[2009년 지방직 7급 12~13번]

04 It is my opinion that Susan and Linda should have been more careful about their
manners in front of their teacher yesterday.

05 'Please' and 'Thank you' are the small change with which we pay our way as social beings. They are the little courtesies by which we keep the machine of life oiled and running sweetly.

2. 보어에「to RV / RVing」가 나온 경우

❖ 다음을 해석하세요. 구문분석집 79P

01 A common mistake in talking to celebrities is to assume that they don't know much about anything else except their occupations.

02 Imagine that it's Saturday and you are to meet your friends at the mall at 12:00.

03 The way to give them positive mind is encouraging each other to participate in activities.

04 They are bringing about an increasing exhaustion of the resources no less of man than of the earth.

05 Six-party talks on North Korea's nuclear program are to resume in Beijing.

06   Birds and bats appear to be similar, but they are different as night and day.

07   The ultimate purpose of product advertising is to let people know the product and make them buy it.

08   One of my most memorable experiences when I was in Venice was wearing a harlequin mask and participating in the carnival.

09   They have proven to be highly adaptable creatures, and their population has not diminished despite the loss of wooded areas.

[2011년 국가직 9급 14번]

10   The time has come for all men to become conscious of the part they can and must play in life if our present civilization is to endure.

11   If you were to store ten bits of information each second of your life, by your 100th birthday, your memory-storage area would be only half full.

12 A common reaction to the proposition that computers will seriously compete with human intelligence is to dismiss this specter based primarily on an examination of contemporary capability.

[2010년 서울시 9급 1~2번]

13 I believe that the cure for these things is partly to be sought in the deliberate control of the currency and of credit by a central institution, and partly in the collection and dissemination of data relating to the business situation including the full publicity, by law if necessary, of all business facts which it is useful to know.

[2010년 국가직 9급 18번]

PATTERN 22 | 주격보어와 목적격보어

1. 주격보어에 명사절이 나온 경우

❖ 다음을 해석하세요.

`구문분석집 83P`

01 What I want to know is whether they will agree or not.

02 One of the most painful circumstances of recent advances in science is that each of them makes us know less than we thought we did.

03 One of the most beguiling aspects of cyberspace is that it offers the ability to connect with others in foreign countries while also providing anonymity.

[2011년 지방직 9급 3번]

04 Despite the fact that many Koreans spend time and money to improve their English proficiency, the sad news is that the majority of them cannot succeed in speaking excellent English unless they have grown up and spent a substantial period of time in English-speaking countries when they were young. [2010년 국회 8급 16번]

2. 목적격보어에 「to RV / RVing / p.p. / RV」가 나온 경우

❖ 다음을 해석하세요.   구문분석집 84P

01   I saw a girl dancing in the middle of the square.

   cf I saw a girl dance in the middle of the square.

02   He was seen to enter the house by me.

03   I found the experience brilliant and it has made me want to succeed and apply for audition after audition.

04   When a little girl was holding a fishing rod on the riverbank, she suddenly felt something and saw the fishing rod bending into a question mark.

05 I got up and found Jenny sitting in her bathrobe at the glass table on the screened porch of our little bungalow, bent over the newspaper with a pen in her hand. [2011년 국가직 7급 3번]

06 The women were busy shopping for Christmas presents but had their shopping bags stolen because they left them in an unlocked car in the parking lot during lunchtime.

07 Officials in the government agency will keep the vicinity of the crash site closed to airboats for another three months to preserve the site in case investigators find reasons to go back to it.

보어의 변형 형태

PATTERN 23 | 「완전자동사 + 보어」가 나온 경우

❖ 다음을 해석하세요.

구문분석집 86P

01 I went away a girl, and have come back a woman.

02 He returned home a completely changed person after spending six months in a mental hospital.

03 Cold and pale lay the Emperor in his bed. But he was not yet dead, although he lay white and still on his bed.

04 This genetic change may cause the child to be born defective in some way.

05 Some people are born weak, but by taking good care of their health, they may become well and strong.

06 A puppy raised apart from other dogs will know how to bark when he gets old enough, but the few children we know of who grew up without human contact grew up almost wholly mute.

❖ 다음을 해석하세요.

구문분석집 88P

01 Don't speak with your mouth full.

02 He could leave the church with all the sin washed out of him.

03 When the students watched the film with an authority figure present, their faces showed only the slightest hints of reaction.

04 The boy and the girl walked in the forest with their heads bent, with birds singing merrily above their heads.

05 Travel is a wonderful educator if it is intelligent travel done with eyes open and mind at work.

06 With processor and Internet-connection speeds doubling every couple of years, the boundaries for games are quickly disappearing.

07 His routine was to sit in the living room with his legs crossed and arms extended while reading a newspaper for a couple of hours in the morning.

08 One simple, effective method is a pill box that looks like a matrix, with days of the week listed along the top and times of the day along the side.

심우철 구문 1000제 [복습종이]

최소시간 X 최대효과 = 초고효율 심우철 합격영어

PART

05

준동사편

PATTERN 25 | 준동사의 해석

1. To RV의 기본 용법 (부정사)

❖ 다음을 해석하세요.

구문분석집 92P

01   To read a newspaper in the room is boring.

02   I want to read a newspaper in the room.

03   The first thing I do in the morning is to read a newspaper in the room.

04   He is to read a newspaper in the room after he finishes the work.

05   The way to learn a language is to practice speaking it as often as possible.

06   To keep children from going out on rainy days is usually difficult for their parents.

07 You had better follow the dentist's advice to have your wisdom teeth taken out.

08 According to Erikson, basic trust involves having the courage to let go of the familiar and take a step toward the unknown.

09 To prevent software from being copied illegally and protect the copyright, above all, software companies should lower the price of their goods to a reasonable price.

2. RVing / p.p.의 기본 용법 (동명사 / 분사 구분하기)

❖ 다음을 해석하세요.   구문분석집 94P

01 Teaching children washing skills at home requires them sensitive care and a little endurance.

02 Teaching children washing skills at home, parents can provide the importance of sanilation.

03 The person teaching children washing skills at home doesn't necessarily have to be the mother.

04   Pretty soon, you will have collected a lot of revealing facts about yourself.

05   Putting a man to death by hanging or electric shock is an extremely cruel form of punishment.

06   The awesome power unleashed by nuclear energy was first demonstrated in the atomic bombs dropped on Hiroshima and Nagasaki.

07   Alexander Bell (1847~1922) also constructed a 'talking head', made out of various synthetic materials, that was able to produce a few distinct sounds.   [2008년 지방직 9급 15번]

3.「전치사 + RVing」가 나온 경우

❖ 다음을 해석하세요.   구문분석집 95P

01   Being in the army is like being in the Boy Scouts, except that the Boy Scouts have adult supervision.

02 On entering the forest, we saw a great number of monkeys, who fled at our approach, and ran up the trees with surprising quickness.

03 In terms of using mental energy creatively, perhaps the most basic difference between people consists in how much attention they have to deal with novelty.

04 The politician's success in converting the people to his way of thinking was largely a result of his persuasive criticisms of the existing order.

05 A basic understanding of the different types of cloning is the key to taking an informed stance on current public policy issues and making the best possible personal decisions.

[2009년 국가직 7급 13번]

06 The White House and congressional leaders worked Monday to align lawmakers from both parties behind their formula for averting a financial meltdown and halting the government's prolific spending habits.

[2011년 국회 8급 7번]

07 When spiders are in danger, they can escape by flying through the air at the end of an instantly made silk dragline.

[2009년 국가직 7급 7번]

PATTERN 26 | 분사구문이 나온 경우

❖ 다음을 해석하세요.

구문분석집 98P

01   Working in a print shop, my coworker and I sometimes forget how complex the equipment

seems to clients.

cf   Communicating with each other by e-mail is becoming more common all over the world.

02   Fueled by a lifelong love of literature, Gonzales has devoted himself to providing people

with more access to literature.

03   Wind and rain continually hit against the surface of the Earth, breaking large rocks into

smaller and smaller particles.

04   Unable to finish college because of a lack of money, he took a job as a playground

instructor earning thirty dollars a week.

05   It is best to let them make their own mistakes and learn from them, always certain that

you will be there to help them recover and start over.

06 Small areas of sand beach are along the New England coast, some created from glacial debris, others built up by the action of ocean storms.

07 Understanding the movements of heavenly bodies and the relationship between angles and distances, medieval travelers were able to create a system of longitude and latitude.

08 Hours of intense negotiations aimed at reopening the government collapsed last night, leaving the White House and congressional Republicans no closer to agreeing on the terms for future budget negotiations than they were a week ago.

09 Medical illnesses such as stroke, a heart attack, cancer, Parkinson's disease, and hormonal disorders can cause depressive illness, making the sick person apathetic and unwilling to care for his or her physical needs, thus prolonging the recovery period.

10 Youth especially tend to take good health for granted and squander it thoughtlessly, little realizing that future success and happiness, and even life itself, are largely influenced and in many instances actually determined by the habits of living acquired during one's developmental years.

PATTERN 27 | 준동사의 의미상의 주어

❖ 다음을 해석하세요.

구문분석집 102P

01 You can make it possible for all men in America and throughout the world, to enjoy these rights to the fullest.

02 Some parents take advantage of their children's longing for goods in order to show their love. Busier parents are tempted to buy their children's love by compensating for the time they did not spend with their children.

03 It being his free afternoon, Frank decided to take a drive in the country.

04 There being no one to go with me, I had to go alone.

05 She is proud of her son's being the brightest in the class.

06   It seems difficult for him to handle such a complicated matter.

07   He introduced the technique of the double image to create the impression of one object being transformed into another.

08   The male moths live longer than the females, the former averaging about four weeks and the latter half that time or a little more.

09   Therefore, the value of the original results not only from its uniqueness but from its being the source from which reproductions are made.

10   Painters want to see the world afresh, and to discard all the accepted notions and prejudices about flesh being pink and apples being yellow or red.

PATTERN 28 | 준동사의 시제와 능동·수동

❖ 다음을 해석하세요.   구문분석집 105P

01   I believe you to have loved her before.

02 Having received no answer from him, I wrote again.

03 He is ashamed of never having been abroad while young.

04 The building is reported to have been badly damaged by fire.

05 The casino in Florida is believed to have generated more than $250 million dollars annually in profit.

06 The allegations about climate scientists are believed to have contributed to a sharp rise in public scepticism about climate change. [2010년 서울시 9급 17번]

07 Having invented machinery, man has become enslaved by it, as he was of old enslaved by the gods created by his imagination.

08 The accumulation of knowledge does not confer any superiority on man if he reaches the end of his life without having deeply evolved as a responsible element of humanity.

PATTERN 29 | 준동사의 관용적 표현

❖ 다음을 해석하세요.   구문분석집 107P

01 He studied very hard only to fail the examination.

   We hurried to the station only to miss the train.

   That frustration has pushed tens of thousands to demonstrate, only to be swiftly quieted when local governments used force and intimidation.

02 It is no use trying to persuade me.

   = It is of no use to try to persuade me.

   = There is no use (in) trying to persuade me.

03 There is no telling what will happen tomorrow.

   = It is impossible to tell what will happen tomorrow.

04 It goes without saying that health is above wealth.

= It is needless to say that health is above wealth.

= It is a matter of course that health is above wealth.

05 This book is worth reading.

= This book is worthy of reading.

= It is worthwhile to read this book.

= It is worthwhile reading this book.

= This book is worthwhile to read.

06 I feel like crying.

= I feel inclined to cry.

07 He came near being killed.

= He narrowly escaped being killed.

08 He watched TV instead of studying.

09 Besides getting a job, I will get married soon.

10 I couldn't help laughing to hear the news.

= I couldn't but laugh to hear the news.

= I could do nothing but laugh to hear the news.

= I couldn't choose but laugh to hear the news.

= I had no choice but to laugh to hear the news.

= There was nothing for it but to laugh to hear the news.

11 I never see this picture without thinking of my mother.

= I never see this picture but I think of my mother.

= When I see this picture, I always think of my mother.

= Whenever I see this picture, I think of my mother.

12 She kept telling herself that she would scold him when he came in.

Take care to keep the wound from being infected.

13 He went to Italy with a view to studying opera.

= He went to Italy for the purpose of studying opera.

14 It is a profession of my own choosing.

15 I make a point of playing tennis every other day.

= I make it a rule to play tennis every other day.

= I am in the habit of playing tennis every other day.

16 The secret is on the point of being revealed.

= The secret is about to be revealed.

17 What do you say to taking a walk in the park?

= What do you think about taking a walk in the park?

= How about taking a walk in the park?

18 She is far from driving a car.

= She is above driving a car.

= She never drives a car.

19   He is busy preparing for the exam.

= He is busy with preparation for the exam.

20   You can have it for the asking.

= You can have it if only you ask.

21   He is too old to fall in love with such a young girl.

= He is so old that he can't fall in love with such a young girl.

22   He looks forward to seeing you in time.

23   A microphone is used to magnify small sounds or to transmit sounds.

He is used to getting up early.

심우철 구문 1000제 [복습종이]

최소시간 X 최대효과 = 초고효율 심우철 합격영어

PART

06

접속사편

PATTERN 30 | 관계대명사 who / which / that의 해석

❖ 다음을 해석하세요.

구문분석집 116P

01   Students develop self-confidence which makes learning and personal growth possible.

cf   He is very candid, which I am not.

He wanted to come, which was impossible.

02   A professor lectured for an hour on the dishonesty of certain dictionary editors who omitted a word from the dictionary because of moral objections.

03   A mathematician is a person whose primary area of study and research is the field of mathematics.

04   In general, parents feel a special kind of love for their own children that they do not feel for other children.

05   Each disc includes a brief introduction to the artist and some interesting information which gives guidance in discovering more about classical music.

06   American inventor Thomas Edison, who had no college degree, nonetheless made himself a classic success story as what we now call a "technologist."

07   History has recorded many instances of creative and imaginative people whose talents were not initially recognized by their contemporaries or whose talents were not evident at an early age.

08   We do not, indeed, know the exact relationship of our physical to our mental being, the extent to which our bodily condition causes our temperament or the exact process by which the brain makes the abstract thing called thought.

09   Too many children here enter the vicious spiral of malnutrition which leads to greater susceptibility to infectious disease, which in turn leads to a greater likelihood of developing malnutrition.

10   The substantial rise in the number of working mothers, whose costs for childcare were not factored into the administration's policymaking, was one of the main reasons that led to the unexpected result at the polls.   [2008년 국가직 9급 9번]

CHAPER

01 형용사절

PATTERN 31 | 관계부사의 해석

❖ 다음을 해석하세요.

구문분석집 120P

01 I love this city of Busan where I was born and raised.

02 A cafe is a small restaurant where people can get a light meal.

03 He finished talking with her at 2 o'clock, when she wanted him to stay a little longer.

04 This is the house where I used to live when I was young.

This is the house which I bought 5 years ago.

05 Because the quality of air is becoming poorer and poorer, I think the time may soon come when we have to take an oxygen tank with us wherever we go.

06 The victim, having agreed to this seemingly innocent request, goes to a room where a number of people—about half a dozen—and the experimenter are seated. [2011년 국가직 7급 5번]

07   One custom that is common at weddings in the United States is throwing rice at the bride and groom as they leave the place where the wedding ceremony has just been held.

[2010년 국가직 9급 10번]

PATTERN 32 | 「전치사 + 관계대명사」의 해석

❖ 다음을 해석하세요.

구문분석집 122P

01   We went to the seashore, on which we found many shells.

02   I bought many books, all of which I have not read.

03   Newspapers and television are said to be the main source from which the public derives its knowledge and information of the facts.

04   We are pumping huge quantities of CO_2 into the atmosphere, almost one-third of which comes from cars.

05   Some stations have automatic gates through which passengers have to pass in order to get to the platforms.

06 I talked with him a long while about our boyhood days, after which we had a good dinner.

I had thought him shy, which he was not.

07 How much one can earn is important, of course, but there are other equally important

considerations, neglect of which may produce frustration in later years.

08 We all need friends with whom we can speak of our deepest concerns, and who provide

us with some things that we can't get from a smaller number of close friends.

09 The company has presented several different alternatives to the group, none of which

was acceptable to all of the members who were present at the time of the meeting.

10 Only recently, in fact, have men conquered, by means of the spoken word, any space

larger than that over which the natural voice will carry, whereas down through the long

course of history, writing has been of inestimable service in bringing men and nations

closer together.

11 The kind of boredom which the person accustomed to drugs experiences when deprived of them is something for which I can suggest no remedy except time. Now what applies to drugs applies also, within limits, to every kind of excitement.

PATTERN 33 | 관계대명사의 생략

❖ 다음을 해석하세요.

구문분석집 125P

01 The child called an orphan is the one whose parents are dead.

02 The man sitting on a bench is the person who I am looking for.

03 Most glaciologists believe it would take another 300 years for the glaciers to melt at the present rate.

[2010년 서울시 9급 17번]

04 One big mistake a lot of teachers make is stigmatizing a student who shows poor performance in school, but in fact has a great talent for something else.

05 One of the most important lessons we can learn is to stop thinking and start doing.

06 Everything we experience and everybody we encounter will carry the scent we hold in our mind.

[2011년 지방직 7급 5번]

07 The type of clothing we wear, the kind of houses in which we live, the type of recreation we enjoy, and the kind of food we eat, are the result of the influences of the groups to which we belong.

08 Mr. President said a freedom agenda would give individuals more power and government less, and promised, as he pushed controversial ideas like revamping Social Security, to reach across party lines.

[2010년 지방직 7급 14번]

09 Since words convey an impression as well as a meaning, a writer must choose his words so that the impression they convey will be suitable to the meaning he intends the reader to understand.

10 Among topics we discussed over lunch was the regrettable habit film directors then had of altering the plot of a novel to suit themselves, to the extent even of changing a sad ending into a happy one.

❖ 다음을 해석하세요.

구문분석집 128P

01 The book is written in such easy English as beginners can understand.

02 He could not resist the temptation, as is often the case with a young man.

03 The ability to sympathize with others reflects the multiple nature of the human being,

his potentialities for many more selves and kinds of experience than any one being could

express.

04 There is no mother but loves her own child.

= There is no mother that does not love her own child.

05 As was the custom with him, he went out for a walk after breakfast.

06 There is not any modern nation but has, in some way, contributed to our science or art

or literature.

07   As life marches on, language must march with it, taking in new words to express new ideas, and leaving behind such words as belong to thoughts and facts that have had their days.

08   He had spoken from impulse rather than from judgement, and as is generally the case with men who do so speak, he had afterwards to acknowledge to himself that he had been imprudent.

09   One of the strange rules which the Spartans had, was that they should speak briefly, and never use more words than were needed.

10   Of course, as is standard in the security business, we would require full guarantees for maintenance and service, and most importantly, a competitive quotation.

11   As is often the case with them, when a wedding anniversary approaches, Korean husbands are forced to entertain their wives with special gifts or trips to destinations the wives want to visit.

12 My mother was also stubborn, as her mother had been before her, and as is often the case with very clever young people, she grew up to find her elders more interesting company than members of her own generation.

PATTERN 35 | 의문사절

❖ 다음을 해석하세요.

구문분석집 132P

01 He asked me which I liked better of the two.

02 I don't know what book to buy for her.

03 Imagine what it would be like to have a machine that cures sick people.

04 I want to know how many visitors our Website receives each day and which pages are visited.

05 They have certain ideas about which foods will increase their athletic ability, help them lose weight, or put them in the mood for romance.

06 Imagine what it must be like for a factory worker to arrive home to his family with the news that he's been laid off.

07 If you cannot decide which of the two things you should do, you are likely to get yourself into trouble by doing neither.

08 The Cyber Crime Institute joined forces with federal law enforcement agencies to find out just how much computer crimes are hurting business, and how far-reaching the problem really is.

09 In general, the context in which the words are spoken or the way in which they are said will tell us which of the possible speaker-meanings is intended.

10 When I go for a walk to some place, I imagine who came there, what kinds of memories they cherished, what they did and talked about there, and so on.

11 With so much to read, and so little time and opportunity in which to read, the simplest and wisest thing we can do is to choose the best books we read.

12 In my hometown, nobody would buy a melon without feeling it and smelling it; and nobody would dream of buying a chicken without knowing which farm it came from and what it ate.

13 Anyone who has used e-mail much has probably noticed how easily one's casual, quickly typed comment can be misunderstood, how suddenly the tone of e-mails can change, and how big conflicts can develop rapidly from a few lines.

14 Utility industry leaders, in determining which of the various types of energy sources to develop, make their decision in the privacy of their room on the basis of profitability, but publicly they justify their choice on the basis of lowered rates and increased safety.

PATTERN 36 ㅣ 「what + S + V」의 해석

❖ 다음을 해석하세요.

구문분석집 136P

01 I was what I was before I ever laid eyes on Peter Kann.

02 The true wealth does not consist in what we have, but in what we are.

03 Man is the only animal that is struck with the difference between what things are and what they ought to be.

04 One of the chief reasons why man alone has made a rapid progress while other animals remain what they used to be is that he came to know how to use fire.

05 Let's leave the matter as it is for a while.

06 I should like to go with you, but as it is, I can't.

07 Reputation is what you seem; character is what you are.

08 To the English, any attempt to appear or any wish to become something other than what one originally is by nature is contemptible, even dishonorable, simply because it is unnatural.

09 To read well is to read with insight and sympathy, to become one with your author, to let him live through you, adding what he is to what you are without losing your own characteristics.

10 We must understand that the dream or vision will always be beyond the accomplishment. This painful separation of what we see we could be and should be and what we are will remain as long as we are human.

11 So long as the mind of man is what it is, it will continue to rejoice in advancing on the unknown throughout the infinite field of the universe; and the tree of knowledge will remain for ever, as it was in the beginning, a tree to be desired to make one wise.

12 The traditional goal of science has been to discover how things are, not how they ought to be, but can a clean-cut distinction between fact and value in the interaction of science and society be sustained any longer?

PATTERN 37 ｜ Wh-ever의 해석

❖ 다음을 해석하세요.

구문분석집 140P

01 Whatever happens, I will do it.

02 Whatever problem you name, you can also name some hoped-for technological solution.

03 This would give us the chance to find information quickly and communicate with others no matter where we are or what we are doing.

04 Whoever comes first will win the prize.

05 Whichever you decide, I'll back you up.

06 We should, therefore, be ready to fight for the right to tell the truth whenever it is threatened.

07 The government recognizes that the economy must remain strong and is willing to provide whatever is needed in order to achieve this excellence.

08 Because the dignity of all human beings was of paramount importance to them, they believed that no matter what kind of work a person did, everyone's contribution to society was of equal value.

09 Their instinct tells them whether they are loved or not, and from those whom they feel to be affectionate, they will put up with whatever strictness results from sincere desire for their proper development.

PATTERN 38 | 「how + 형/부」와 「however + 형/부」의 해석

❖ 다음을 해석하세요.

구문분석집 143P

01 However hard you may try, you cannot do it in a week.

02 If others see how angry, hurt, or hateful you become when they tell you the truth, they will avoid telling it to you at all costs.

03 There is no living plant or animal, however common it may be, that will not repay study, and provide, if intelligently observed, quite an interesting story.

04 However intelligent and thoughtful a person may be, he or she cannot make wise choices unless he or she knows the facts about his or her problem.

05 No matter how much time you have squandered in the past, the next hour that comes your way will be perfect, unspoiled, and ready for you to make the very best of it.

06 We're confident that once you see how enjoyable our software is, and how productive it can make you, you'll join the ranks of our more than 1 million satisfied customers!

07 A study in the August 6 *New England Journal of Medicine* shows how difficult it can be for kids to avoid foods that trigger allergies — and how the consequences of a slip can be deadly.

08 However well any article may be written, and however well any speech may be reported, there is a charm in the spoken word, in the utterance of the living man, which no beauty of style can imitate, and no arrangement of words can equal.

09 Instilling knowledge is obviously not irrelevant to them, but their concerns with it are determined by the much more important question of how one enables a student to become an autonomous thinker, able to see conventional ideas critically. [2009년 지방직 7급 9~10번]

PATTERN 39 | that의 용법

❖ 다음을 해석하세요.

구문분석집 146P

01 That is my English teacher, Shimson.

02 That firm is the biggest in the country.

03 I lost my watch that my father had given to me.

04 I thought that he could finish the work before dark.

05 She is so kind that we cannot hate her.

06 Should a bird fly into your house, it would be an indication that important news is on the way.

07 Bullying has become so extreme and so common that many teens just accept it as part of highschool life in the 90s.

08 Their primitiveness would only confirm our sense that we live in a fundamentally different world, one of constant, instant access to information.

09 For example, *US News and World Report* shows that a picture of the "typical" millionaire is an individual who has worked eight to ten hours a day for thirty years and is still married to his or her high school or college sweetheart.

10 The fact that people are no longer tied to specific places for functions such as working or studying means that there is a huge drop in demand for traditional, private, enclosed spaces such as offices or classrooms, and simultaneously a huge rise in demand for semi-public spaces that can be informally appropriated to ad-hoc workspaces.

[2010년 서울시 9급 12~14번]

PATTERN 40 | if / whether의 해석

❖ 다음을 해석하세요.   구문분석집 149P

01   If you finish your studies at university, I will teach you all that you need.

02   Can I find out if planning permission is required before I submit an application?

03   When you brainstorm, you do not think about whether the idea is good or bad or whether
your writing is correct.

04   Napoleon was rarely, if ever, deceived in regard to a man's actual ability.

05   Few people, if any, are always sustained by unselfish motives, and few or none are
beyond their influence.

06   Whether we receive from society blessing or cursing, a smile or a sneer, the warm hand
or the cold shoulder, will altogether depend on our own attitude with regard to it.

07 If you ask somebody if their parents are living in the area and they frown or back off slightly, their visual cues show that you've probably touched a sensitive subject area for them.

08 The executives should estimate their debt-to-income ratios to see whether they run the risk of becoming insolvent. [2010년 국가직 9급 4번]

09 The argument about when apes end and humans begin is paralleled by arguments about whether various forms of early narrative should or shouldn't be described as 'novels'. [2010년 국회 8급 1~2번]

PATTERN 41 | as의 해석

❖ 다음을 해석하세요.

구문분석집 152P

01   As spring comes, the birds move northward.

02   As we grow older, we come to know the limit of our ability.

03   "How well it would be," said Seneca, "if men would but exercise their brains as they do their bodies, and take as much pains for virtue as they do for pleasure."

04   Just as printing opened a new age, so has broadcasting made possible a new era of international thinking and education.

05   Just as the same body can be dressed in different clothes, so the same thought can be expressed in different languages.

06 Just as ability to understand the spoken word is necessary if you are to comprehend a play, you cannot fail to profit by the knowledge of the words of opera.

[2008년 지방직 9급 12번]

07 Agriculture is responsible for providing food for a growing population and as it becomes clear that yields cannot continue to rise without limit, the sustainability of agricultural practices becomes an increasingly important question.

[2008년 국가직 7급 12번]

PATTERN 42 | 「as ~ as」 구문

❖ 다음을 해석하세요.

구문분석집 154P

01 He ran as fast as possible.

= He ran as fast as he could.

02 He is as brave as any soldier in the world.

= He is as brave a soldier as ever lived.

03 He went as far as Chicago.

04 As(So) far as I know, there was nobody to be satisfied.

05   Each year, as many as two hundred towns in the United States just disappear from the map as far as the Postal Service is concerned.

06   His face was washed, and he was dressed in a nice suit of clothes; and then he was as handsome a young man as ever walked along the streets of London.

07   Setting up marine protected areas to reduce impacts generally on coral reefs to allow them to recover as quickly as possible from unavoidable bleaching would likely help.

08   One principle asserts that social work clients have the right to hold and express their own opinions and to act on them, as long as doing so does not infringe on the rights of others.

09   Tales of frustration abound and serve as a reminder that observation of brief astronomical phenomena, no matter how predictable, can often depend on luck as much as anything.

❖ 다음을 해석하세요.   구문분석집 156P

01   All but he are present.

02   He is all but dead.

03   He will do anything but the work.

04   He is anything but a poet.

05   When you feel compelled to deal with other people's issues, your goal of becoming more

     peaceful becomes all but impossible.

06   All but two of her employees work full-time, and receive benefits including health insurance.

07   Thai officials have all but stopped issuing licenses for tuk tuk taxis because of pollution

     worries and a poor accident record.

08 I know, as does the Minister, that we can be anything but certain that there will not be further successful terrorist incidents.

09 From the rising of the sun nothing was in sight but a waste of waters on the left, a desert plain on the right, and the rugged heights of Carmel dim in the distance.

10 If you're warming up for a typical relaxed five-mile run, you don't have to do anything but start slowly, or start with a minute or two of walking before breaking into a run.

11 In the twenty-four oil paintings and twelve etchings Rembrandt did of himself, all but one show him with his right eye looking straight ahead and his left eye looking outwards.

PATTERN 44 | 상관 접속사

❖ 다음을 해석하세요.

구문분석집 159P

01 The secret lies not in finding smart ways to do more, but in how we manage the relationship between the things we have to do and the time available to do them in.

02 Upon closer analysis, "emerging" countries are not only vastly different from one another; they are also composed of numerous unique individuals and communities.

03 The function of the historian is neither to love the past nor to emancipate himself from the past, but to master and understand it as the key to the understanding of the present.

[2009년 국가직 9급 8번]

04 Then it is the belief in equality, not in the sense that everybody is alike or equally gifted, which is obviously untrue, but in the sense that everyone should have certain basic opportunities.

[2011년 지방직 7급 8번]

05 Men are more likely to view the community in terms of production, whereas women see it, not only as a place where people can earn their livelihood, but also as a place where all can attain and enjoy the good life.

06 Optimist here means not that person an American writer once defined as "a proponent of the doctrine that black is white" but someone who can let his or her eyes sweep the world and come to rest with a mote of hope in the haze of sorrow.

PATTERN 45 | 「not ~ until」 구문

❖ 다음을 해석하세요.   구문분석집 161P

01   He did not turn up until the Sunday service was held.

= It was not until the Sunday service was held that he turned up.

= Not until the Sunday service was held did he turn up.

02   We had not waited half an hour before the fog began to clear up and a strange scene presented itself.

03   It was not until 1962 that the first communications satellite, Telstar, went up.

04   Not until his life was over were his works appreciated by people in general and purchased at high prices.

05   It was not until the shadow of the forest had crept far across the lake and the darkening waters were still that we rose reluctantly to put dishes in the basket and started on our homeward journey.

06 Although the date has long been celebrated as a day for exchanging love messages, it was not until the 18th century that it became commercialized, with cards, chocolates, and small gifts exchanged between people who bear each other either strong friendship or affection.

07 The more carefully nature has been studied, the more widely has order been found to prevail, while what seemed disorder has proved to be nothing but complexity, until, at present, no one is so foolish as to believe that anything happens by chance, or that there are any real accidents, in the sense of events which have no cause.

PATTERN 46 | 시간·조건의 부사절

❖ 다음을 해석하세요.   구문분석집 163P

01 No sooner had I finished an elaborate car washing than the rain began to fall.

02 I will forgive you, if only you apologize to me in a polite manner.

03 Once there is a threat to its supply, however, water can quickly become the only thing that matters.

04 Given the destructive results, do these beliefs make sense?

05 Books can be renewed once for the original loan period unless they are on reserve.

06 Given this situation, these people have striven to conserve the wild plants growing in Korea.

07 No matter what road is chosen, the travelers who started from different valleys will all meet on the top of the mountain, provided they keep on ascending.

08 Given the general knowledge of the health risks of smoking, it is no wonder that the majority of smokers have tried at some time in their lives to quit.   [2008년 지방직 9급 9번]

09 The rapidity of the increase of scientific knowledge, in the nineteenth and twentieth centuries, is apt to give students and teachers the impression that no sooner is a problem stated than the answer is forthcoming.

PATTERN 47 | 목적·결과의 부사절

❖ 다음을 해석하세요.

구문분석집 165P

01 He spoke so rapidly that we could not clearly understand him.

02 All I ask in return is that you take good enough care of yourself so that someday you can do the same thing for someone else.

03 We often hear that it is one thing to hear, and it is another to see. So we must be very careful lest we should believe lightly what other people say.

04 Parents of vocational high school students even press schools to add more general subjects to their curricula so that their children may have some hope of getting into college.

05 I have played Wizard for so many years that I may as well continue the part a little longer.

06 This pretense of public spirit is so consistently maintained that most of these men come presently to believe in their own professions' worth.   [2011년 국가직 7급 12~13번]

PATTERN 48 | 이유·양보의 부사절

❖ 다음을 해석하세요.   구문분석집 167P

01 Seeing that you lied to me, I can't trust you any longer.

02 What with fatigue and what with hunger, the old man fell down.

03 Although the new features had looked attractive separately, the entire assembly shocked him, for he found that he had been changed into an ugly camel.

04   Now that the court is dry, we can play tennis.

05   I have had the opportunity to look them over, and I feel that they show considerable promise, despite your youth and lack of experience in this genre.

심우철 구문 1000제 [복습종이]

최소시간 X 최대효과 = 초고효율 심우철 합격영어

PART

07

나머지
세상의 모든 구문

PART

07

나머지 세상의 모든 구문

PATTERN 49 | 삽입

❖ 다음을 해석하세요.

구문분석집 170P

01 Ignoring his advice, I wasted my time and continued to paint what I thought was popular.

02 Spiders, though not generally popular, are true friends of man, and some scientists believe that human life could not exist without them.

03 His opinion, it seems to me, is not worth considering.

04 The man who I thought was his father proved to be a perfect stranger.

05 Disharmony enters our relationships when we try to impose our values on others by wanting them to live by what we feel is "right," "fair," "good," "bad," and so on.

06 We often hear stories of ordinary people who, if education had focused on creativity, could have become great artists or scientists.

07 When we are employed in reading a great and good author, we ought to consider ourselves as searching after treasures, which, if well and regularly laid up in the mind, will be of use to us on various occasions in our lives.

08 The smell of gasoline going into a car's tank during a refueling stop, when combined with the fact that each day nearly a billion gallons of crude oil are refined and used in the United States, can allow our imagination to spread outward into the vast global network of energy trade and politics.

PATTERN 50 | 비교급·원급 해석

❖ 다음을 해석하세요.

구문분석집 173P

01 This may mean going to bed an hour earlier, but having an extra hour in the morning is so much more productive than staying up an hour later at the end of the day.

02 According to the study, violence and property crimes were nearly twice as high in sections of the buildings where vegetation was low, compared with the sections where vegetation was high.

03 People seem to be more motivated by the thought of losing something than by the thought of gaining something of equal value.

04 Comparing the remembered carefree past with his immediate problems, the mature man thinks that troubles belong only to the present.

05 Researchers studied men who have experienced low level inflammation of the arteries for several years, and found them to be three times as likely to suffer heart attack and twice as likely to have strokes as normal men.

06 In this vein, physicians' advice to smokers, describing the number of years to be gained if they do quit, might be somewhat ineffective as compared with advice describing the number of years of life to be lost if they do not quit.

07 A study showed that if schoolchildren eat fruit, eggs, bread and milk before going to school, they will learn more quickly and be able to concentrate on their lessons for a longer period of time than if their breakfast is poor.

08 Over the past few years I have consistently preached that nonviolence demands that the means we use must be as pure as the ends we seek.

09 Some readers underline the page as they read, but I find that a page which I have underlined cannot give me so many fresh impressions as one which has no marks on it.

PATTERN 51 | the + 비교급, the + 비교급

❖ 다음을 해석하세요.

구문분석집 176P

01 The more globalized the world becomes in the 21st century, the more important English will be.

02 The more contact a group has with another group, the more likely it is that objects or ideas will be exchanged.

03 The stronger the vibration of the sound, the greater the pressure difference between the high and the low, and the louder the sound.

04 The sooner a consumer throws away the object he has bought and buys another, the better it is for the producer.

05 The faster jets go, the hotter they get and the more fuel they use. The more fuel they consume, the shorter their period of flight.

06 The more traveling there is, the more will culture and way of life tend everywhere to be standardized and therefore the less educative will travel become.

07 We are so familiar with the fact that man ages, that people have for years assumed that the process of losing vigour with time, of becoming more likely to die the older we get, was something self-evident, like the cooling of a hot kettle or the wearing out of a pair of shoes.

❖ 다음을 해석하세요.

구문분석집 178P

01 Often what they seek is not so much profound knowledge as quick information.

02 Nonetheless, most New Yorkers don't even own guns, much less carry one around with them.

03 They lived no less successful lives than those whose names have become familiar to the world.

04 Melancholy is caused less by the failure to achieve great ambitions or desires than by the inability to perform small necessary acts.

05 He tried to soothe his wife by giving her a present rather than taking her out for a walk.

06 He exists less by the actions performed during his life than by the wake he leaves behind him like a shooting star.

07 If you must give your child a credit card, the experts say, make sure it has a pre-set limit of no more than a thousand dollars, and teach your children that the card is to be used only in emergencies.

08 Rather, he said, it represents no less than a new paradigm for the way museums in general collect art and interact with one another.   [2010년 지방직 7급 5번]

09 The problems of today have become so complex that a superficial knowledge is inadequate to enable the cultivated layman to grasp them all, much less to discuss them.

10 I have learned that success is to be measured less by the position that one has reached in life than by the obstacles which he has overcome while trying to succeed.

11 Within no longer than a decade or two, the probability of spending part of one's life in a foreign culture will exceed the probability a hundred years ago of ever leaving the town in which one was born.

12 No minority of any ethnicity had ever looked beyond the scarce representation of a few Senators and seen anything that suggested that the doorknob of the Oval Office could be opened by anything other than the hand of a middle-aged white male. [2011년 지방직 9급 13번]

13 As we grow older, we discover that what seemed at the time an absorbing interest was in reality an appetite or passion which had swept over us and passed on, until at last we come to see that our life has no more continuity than a pool in rocks filled by the tide with foam and then emptied.

PATTERN 53 | 다양한 최상급 표현

❖ 다음을 해석하세요.   구문분석집 182P

01 He is as qualified as any man in the company.

02 Nowhere is prey detection with this sense better developed than in sharks.

03 The highest reward for a person's toil is not what they get for it, but what they become by it.

04   He always works hardest in the office.

05   The noblest face reveals potential evil overcome; the vilest potential good suppressed.

06   Although gestures seem rather natural to us and almost inherently meaningful, they are as arbitrary as any word in any language.

07   Of all the travelers who have journeyed to that enchanted realm of Once Upon a Time, none has come back with treasures more glistening than Hans Christian Andersen.

08   Few writers have equaled Willa Cather in understanding the violent clash that occurred in the United States when the gentle, hopeful immigrants from the Old World struck the rigorous, inhospitable prairies of the New.

❖ 다음을 해석하세요.

구문분석집 184P

01 There was little change for the better.

02 He is anything but a scholar.

03 Archimedes was the last man to say that anything was impossible.

04 It is so far from being true that men are naturally equal.

05 Who knew he was an industrial spy?

    = Nobody knew he was an industrial spy.

06 It your success is not on your own terms, if it looks good to the world but does not feel

    good in your soul, it is not success at all.

07 I reminded myself that since Harry had surely dressed her down already, the last thing she needed was yet another scolding.

08 The failure of the summit may be a blessing in disguise, because when it comes to dealing with climate change, the last thing we need right now is yet another empty agreement and yet more moral posturing.

[2010년 국가직 7급 6번]

PATTERN 55 | 부분부정·전체부정·이중부정

❖ 다음을 해석하세요.

구문분석집 186P

01 If I had told you that the ocean is full of sharks, you might have panicked and none of us would have swum and reached this beach.

02 She never passed her old home but she thought of the happy years she had spent there with her family.

03 Shoes have not always served such a purely functional purpose, however, and the requirements of fashion have dictated some curious designs, not all of which made walking easy.

04 Without the sense of touch, we could not feel any difference between rough and smooth surfaces.

05 Boys cannot all become great men, but they can all become good men.

06 We cannot study the lives of great men without noticing how often an apparent misfortune was for them an exceedingly fortunate thing.

07 Today, many people believe in "fair trade." I'm surprised that I can't go to my university, supermarket, or watch my favorite food television program without everyone complimenting the ethical superiority of the fair-trade option.

나머지 세상의 모든 구문

PATTERN 56 | 대명사 해석

❖ 다음을 해석하세요.

구문분석집 188P

01 It is one thing to work for money, and it is quite another to have your money work for you.

02 What a blanket always does is to prevent heat from passing through one side of it to the other.

03 The cycles of Western economies during the 20th century had a significant impact on the prevalence of objects that emphasized design over styling — and the other way around.

04 The truth is quite the other way around.

05 Of the two men, I prefer the former to the latter.

06 Does the earth revolve around the sun, or is it the other way around?

07 Passing your driving test is one thing, and being a good driver is another.

08 In fact, it's more likely that high productivity creates job satisfaction rather than the other way around.

09 The latter is said to migrate in large numbers, while the former in small numbers or individually.

10 Some of their artificial mothers were made of cold, hard wire while the others were made of warm, soft towel cloth.

PATTERN 57 | 명-RVing / 명-p.p.의 해석

❖ 다음을 해석하세요.

구문분석집 191P

01 The company reduced its water use by installing automatic faucets and water-saving toilets, saving 152,000 dollars.

02 Some Korean artists suggest that the process of making hanji, hand-made Korean paper, reflects human life.

03 As I turned the corner off the tree-lined street, I realized the whole house was shining with light.

04 Over the last few decades, biologists have found that whales, elephants, and some other animals also use this extremely low-pitched sound to communicate.

05 The number of people under 70 dying from smoking-related diseases is larger than the total number of deaths caused by breast cancer, AIDS, and traffic accidents.

06 Founded in 1960 to gain greater control over the price of oil, OPEC consists of the main Arabic oil-producing countries.   [2009년 국가직 7급 1번]

07 While activists prepare to unfurl protest banners, politicians are scrambling for a face-saving way to declare the summit a success.   [2010년 국가직 7급 6번]

08 In general terms, tablet PC refers to a slate-shaped mobile computer device, equipped with a touchscreen or stylus to operate the computer.   [2011년 국가직 9급 3번]

09 The well-born young Athenians who gathered around Socrates found it quite paradoxical that their hero was so intelligent, so brave, so honorable, so seductive — and so ugly.

[2009년 국가직 9급 16번]

10 Molecules found in red wine have for the first time been shown to mimic the life-extending effects of calorie restriction, a finding that could help researchers develop drugs that lengthen life and prevent or treat aging-related diseases.

PATTERN 58 | 「be + 형용사 + 전치사」 / V + one's way

❖ 다음을 해석하세요.

구문분석집 194P

01 She was certain that the young man had gone mad.

02 If you don't want to find yourself on thin ice, you must be sure of your facts.

03 Plants that stay inside all winter will be glad of all the light they can get.

04 When we are not too anxious about happiness and unhappiness but devote ourselves to the strict and faithful performance of duty, then happiness comes of itself.

05 It is a common prejudice that whales live only in the cold, open water of the oceans, and most of my fellow countrymen from Greece are not aware of the fact that bottlenose whales live right in front of their noses.

[2010년 국가직 7급 9~10번]

06 The division of Europe into a number of independent states, connected, however, with each other by the general resemblance of religion, language, and manners, is productive of the most beneficial consequences to the liberty of mankind.

07 She made her way through the crowd.

08 They cut their way into the jungle.

09 She elbowed her way through the crowd.

10 It is easier to go with the tide than to try to force one's way against public opinion.

11   He found his way to Chicago.

12   The blind man groped his way along the corridor.

13   He worked his way through college.

14   Frank Sinatra said that he would keep his way even in bad times.

15   To pay his way through school, he taught classes at Yale.

16   She wins her way to be loved by her mother.

심우철 구문 1000제 [복습종이]

최소시간 X 최대효과 = 초고효율 심우철 합격영어

부록

직독직해의
법칙

심우철 구문 1000제 [복습종이]

직독직해의 법칙

원리 01 | 구의 개념을 잘 잡아라

❖ 다음을 해석하세요.

본책 190P

01   The girl will stay at home during Christmas.

02   One of the most important tasks of the teacher is to help his students.

03   Everyone in the new city likes John for his industry.

04   He sent me a message that he would come back soon.

05   Sleep enables the body to remove the harmful products.

06   The drop of the test scores over the past few decades supports this view.

07   This sense of being separate from the rest of the universe, often leads to a feeling of loneliness.

08   The computer will drive the car down the road at a speed of 120 miles an hour.

09   A number of listening tests contain short statements in the form of instructions or dictations.

10   A ray of light passing through the center of a thin lens keeps its original direction.

11   A young man may spend 30 minutes watching a leaf carried down a sidewalk by a gentle breeze.

원리 02 | 영어는 중요한 것이 문장 앞부분에 나온다

❖ 다음을 해석하세요.   본책 194P

01   Park Ji-sung fights for the ball with an Angolan player during their international friendly football match at Sangam World Stadium in South Korea.

02   In China it can be illegal to talk to a foreign press about the protest that has taken place in the country.

03   The Eskimos resemble a group of Asian people.

The Eskimos living in the Arctic today resemble a group of Asian people known as Mongolians.

04   There was a tragic piece of news that a very fat neighbor dieted herself to death.

There was a tragic piece of news that a very fat neighbor, whose sole wish was to lose weight, dieted herself to death.

05   She paused at the restaurant window, wrapping her coat collar high around her neck.

원리 03 | 직독직해를 위한 6가지 *skills*

Skill 01 주어가 긴 경우, 동사 앞에서 주어를 다시 한 번 해석한다.

❖ 다음을 해석하세요.   본책 196P

01   Researchers who studied behaviors on people working at least 30 hours a week found the incredible facts.

02   A series of high-profile cases involving the loss of computer discs by Government departments has left many police forces having to rethink the way they carry confidential information.

To RV가 문장 맨 앞에 길게 나온 경우

❖ 다음을 해석하세요.

본책 198P

01 To think of the future in relation to the present is essential to civilization.

02 To be brave especially in front of women is a lifelong goal for most of the gentlemen.

03 To get some wisdom from superstitions, you need a good education from the intelligent people.

04 To help a stranger find a street or a railway station, or to answer any questions that he may ask, have you ever stopped walking to spare your time for him?

05 To be the best writing, concrete words are better than abstract ones, and the shortest way of saying anything is always the best.

RVing가 문장 맨 앞에 길게 나온 경우

❖ 다음을 해석하세요.   본책 201P

01 Predicting interview questions and thinking about answers in advance will help you feel more confident.

02 Downloading music illegally from the Web is causing serious damage to the music industry.

03 Reducing stress, through meditation, exercise, deep breathing, yoga, or whatever works for you, may help ease your symptoms.

04 Keeping in mind that they are dependent on the other people for having happy lives, the rich should be willing to help the poor.

05 Eating the cherry pie, I struck several pits and nearly broke a tooth.

06 Working with researchers from Chicago University, Bronks has designed its products to meet the special biomechanical needs of men and women.

Skill 03 콤마(,) 다음에 **RVing/p.p.**가 나온 경우, 앞에 〈그러면서〉라는 말을 넣어준다.

❖ 다음을 해석하세요.　　　　　　　　　　　　　　　　　　　　　　　本책 203P

01 Wind and rain continually hit against the surface of the Earth, breaking large rocks into smaller and smaller particles.

02 A tsunami is strong enough to destroy objects in its path, often reducing buildings to their foundations and scouring exposed ground to the bedrock.

03 Schools should stick to academics, leaving moral education to the parents and the community.

Skill 04 〈핵심어 + 수식어〉의 경우, 수식어구(형용사/부정사/분사/관계사)가 길 때는 〈그런데 그 명사는/그 명사란〉으로 해석한다.

❖ 다음을 해석하세요.　　　　　　　　　　　　　　　　　　　　　　　본책 204P

01 Employers look for employees supporting each other, taking pride in their work, and encouraging a pleasant working environment.

02 We simply do not have the technology to travel to the nearest star in a human lifetime.

Skill 05 관계대명사는 〈그런데 그 명사〉로 해석하고, 관계부사는 〈그런데 그 명사에(서)/ (으)로〉라고 해석한다.

❖ 다음을 해석하세요. `본책 205P`

01 Rueven has developed a program that involves hundreds of hours of special tutoring.

02 Our incredible growth rate leads to a continuous recruitment of ambitious programmer analysts who have the desire to make a significant contribution to an expanding company.

03 The United States of America became the place where millions of expatriates from all European countries were searching for free economic evolvement.

Skill 06 문장 맨 앞에 접속사가 나온 경우, 두 번째(주절) 주어 앞에서 그 접속사를 다시 한 번 해석해주면 두 문장을 매끄럽게 이을 수 있다.

❖ 다음을 해석하세요. `본책 207P`

01 Although her daughter waited upon her day and night with loving care, she got worse and worse, until at last there was no hope left.

02 Because diamonds can only be scratched by other diamonds, it maintains its polish extremely well, keeping its luster over long periods of time.

Staff

Writer	심우철
Director	박진우
Researcher	김지훈 / 김세빈 / 정규리
Design	강현구
Manufacture	김승훈
Marketing	유주심 / 윤대규

발행일   2021년 7월 1일 (개정 2판 1쇄)

Copyright ⓒ 2021
by Shimson English Lab.

내용문의 http://cafe.naver.com/shimson2000